TECHNOLOGICAL
DUBLIN

TECHNOLOGICAL
UNIVERSITY DUBLIN

Donated to

**Visual Art Degree
Sherkin Island**

beautiful boxes

beautiful boxes

APPLE

CONTENTS

1
Papercrafts

2
Découpage

3
Paint effects

4
Natural choice

5
Fabulous fabric

6
Design in 3-D

A Quarto Book

Published by the Apple Press
6 Blundell Street
London N7 9BH

ISBN 1-85076-727-0

This book was designed and produced by
Quarto Publishing plc
6 Blundell Street
London N7 9BH

Senior editor Eileen Cadman
Copy editor Barbara Cheney
Art editor Toni Toma
Designer John Grain
Photographers Martin Norris, Les Weis,
Laura Wickenden
Art director Moira Clinch
Editorial director Mark Dartford

Typeset by Central Southern Typesetters, Eastbourne
Manufactured by Regent Publishing Services Ltd,
Hong Kong
Printed by Leefung-Asco Printers Ltd, China

Introduction

Much of the fun of decorating boxes is in revamping old boxes that have seen better days. It is surprisingly simple to make new, designer-style containers very economically. Use your creations to store jewellery, needlework tools, photographs and letters or to hide a special gift. All of the boxes make lovely gifts themselves.

Equipment

You probably already possess most of the basic equipment needed to decorate boxes. Always work on a clean, flat surface, and keep sharp implements, paints and glues beyond the reach of children.

Drawing tools
Use an HB pencil for drawing. Keep pencils sharpened to a point for accuracy or use a propelling pencil. Always use a ruler and set square when drawing squares and rectangles so that the angles are accurate. Use a compass to draw circles.

Cutting tools
Sharp, pointed scissors are the most versatile for craftwork. Choose a pair that feels comfortable. For cutting detailed shapes a small pair is best. For découpage, embroidery, dissecting or manicure scissors are more suitable. Curved manicure scissors are useful for cutting curves. Use dressmaking scissors for cutting fabric but not to cut paper as it will blunt the blades. Embroidery scissors are best for intricate fabric motifs and threads.

   Craft knives and scalpels give a neat cut on paper and card. Always use them on a cutting mat and replace the blades frequently, as a blunt blade will tear paper. Do not use a craft knife to cut tissue paper as it will rip. Cut straight edges against a metal ruler. Use wire cutters or an old pair of scissors to cut metals.

Adhesives
The large variety of materials that can be used to decorate boxes means that more than one type of glue may be needed for a project. Always follow the manufacturer's instructions carefully and test first on any scraps. To distribute the glue evenly use a plastic spreader or thin strip of card. For intricate areas use a cocktail stick.

   PVA (polyvinyl acetate) medium is a very versatile glue. It is a non-toxic white solution that dries to a clear finish. Use it for sticking paper and fabric and for making papier mâché models.

Super glue (strong epoxy resin) is very strong and will stick paper, card, metals, wood, fabric and some plastics. Always handle super glue carefully: a gel glue is easier to apply than the liquid form when only a small amount of glue is needed. Store super glue upright to prevent clogging.

All-purpose household glue and rubber glue are both suitable for sticking materials such as paper, card, beads and pressed flowers. If you plan to do a lot of craftwork, buy a glue gun. It is quick and easy to use and suitable for many materials.

Painting tools

For best results use the paintbrush recommended for the type of paint that you are using. Good quality artist's brushes are worth the expense. Use a fine paintbrush for detailed work. Always clean brushes well immediately after use. Use a stencilling brush for stencilling.

Paint can also be applied with a sponge or spattered with an old toothbrush for random speckled effects. A badger-hair varnishing brush is best for applying varnish, but a flat paintbrush would also be suitable.

Materials

Choosing boxes

Choosing a suitable box to decorate needs a little thought. For example, what is the purpose of the box? Will it have a practical use for storage, or is it to be purely decorative? Do you intend it as a gift for someone? What should it be made of? A box for storing stationery or toys may need to be hardwearing, so would metal or wood be the best material? Jewellery boxes are handled more carefully, so a variety of materials could be used. Purely ornamental boxes can be delicate or hard-wearing.

Look out for interesting boxes at junk shops or revitalize old seed boxes and shoeboxes. Plain cardboard and wooden box "blanks" are available from craft shops ready for decoration.

The box needs to be suited to its proposed decoration. Be sure that a lid that slips over the top of the box will still fit once it has been covered with paper, fabric or paint. The lid of a wooden box can be sanded inside to make it fit.

Preparation

Secondhand boxes may need some preparation first. Sandpaper wooden boxes to even out the surface and to prepare for painting. Fill any cracks with wood filler, leave to dry, then sand down.

To prepare a metal or enamel box, clean off any rust with a wire brush and wet-and-dry paper, then apply a coat of metal primer.

Paper and card

There is a huge choice of paper available. Giftwrap paper is an inexpensive way of transforming a plain box. Even corrugated card can be used creatively. Art shops and specialist paper shops stock some beautiful examples such as wood veneer papers, textured and handmade papers which, although expensive, will make a simple project very special.

Stencil board has a waxed coating which means that it can be re-used. Stencils can also be cut from acetate or card. Mounting board is made of layers of compressed card. It must be cut with a craft knife. Use mounting board to add three-dimensional details.

Paints

Boxes to be painted may need undercoat. Use acrylic gesso or emulsion paint for water-based paints and an oil-based primer for oil-based paints.

Craft paints are very versatile and come in a wide choice of finishes. Acrylic and poster paints are available in a large range of colours.

Although oil paints are slow-drying, the result is worth waiting for. Indian inks give interesting translucent effects. Relief and glitter paints come in bottles with a thin nozzle to apply the paint which dries slightly embossed. Metallic powders can be rubbed into wood or clay to colour the surface.

Spray paints give an even covering of paint and can be used for stencilling.

Natural materials

The garden can provide a wonderful choice of materials to use for decorating boxes.

The seashore is another great source of exciting natural materials. Shells, driftwood and sea-smoothed pebbles work well together. Specialist shell shops sell exotic shells and accessories.

Raffia can be woven or tied to create ethnic styles. Both natural and dyed shades can be bought. Raffia, string and cord can be dyed with fabric dyes.

Needlework materials

Beautiful fabrics will transform a plain box very quickly. As only small amounts of fabric are needed, search offcuts and remnants at fabric stores.

Your fabric-covered box can be decorated with a huge choice of materials. Beads, sequins, ribbons and tassels will give a flamboyant finishing touch.

Modelling materials

Stylish boxes can be made from scratch using fine metal foil or decorated with motifs modelled from clay. Air-drying clay is simple to use and can be painted.

Polymer clay is available in many colours, it is hardened by baking in an oven for a short time. Papier mâché pulp can be bought in dry form that is then mixed with water, or it can be made by hand.

Salt dough is now enjoying a welcome revival. Made from flour, salt and water, the dough is baked slowly in a cool oven. It can then be painted. Varnished well and kept away from moisture it can last for years.

La lune blanche
Luit dans les bois;
De chaque branche
Part une voix
Sous la ramée...
Ô bien-aimée.

L'étang reflète,
Profond miroir,
La silhouette
Du saule noir
Où le vent pleure...
Rêvons: c'est l'heure.

Verlaine

Papercrafts

Papercrafts are a good starting point as paper and card are some of the most economical materials.

Stick on cut or torn coloured papers. Recycle newspapers to make papier mâché pulp and mould into unusual sculptural motifs.

Marquetry magic

This is an inexpensive version of the beautiful wood craft of marquetry. Wood veneer papers are cut and glued to resemble fine inlaid wood.

You will need . . .

- Round wooden box
- Wood veneer papers in three colours
- Pencil
- Ruler
- Tracing paper
- Scissors
- Masking tape
- PVA medium
- Flat paintbrush

1 With a pencil, draw round the box lid on tracing paper and cut out. Draw a simple design such as this nautical compass within the circumference. Place the tracing face down on the wrong side of one of the papers and secure in place with masking tape. Check that the wood grain is lying in a suitable direction then trace the outline to transfer it. Use a ruler for straight lines.

2 In this way, transfer each section of the design to the papers then carefully cut them out.

3 Tape the tracing right side up at one edge of the lid. Using a paintbrush, apply PVA medium to the paper sections and stick to the lid. Work outwards from the centre and slip each piece under the tracing to help with correct positioning. Add a coordinating border around the lid rim if you wish. Coat with varnish if the box is to be handled often.

Safari **stripes**

Torn strips of leatherette paper are applied to a cardboard box to achieve this stunning zebra-skin effect. Experiment with other colourways to make tiger and leopard-skin boxes.

You **will need . . .**

- Cardboard box
- Black and white leatherette paper
- Scissors
- PVA medium
- Flat paintbrush

1 The lid: cut white leatherette paper into wavy and curved strips 1–2cm (⅜–¾in) wide. Cut the ends of the strips to a rounded point. Using a paintbrush, apply PVA medium to a section of the lid and stick on a strip. Apply more PVA medium and continue to cover the lid, overlapping the strips.

2 Cover the box in the same way. Snip the excess paper at the corners. Stick the paper to the inside of the box and under it with the PVA medium.

3 Cut wavy and curved strips of black leatherette paper as in step 1. Apply PVA medium to a section of the box and stick on a black strip. Apply more strips using the same method to create a random design. Decorate the other sides and the lid in the same way. Leave to dry.

Cactus pencil box

This fun pencil box is a good project to do with a child. You can buy ready-made papier mâché pulp very cheaply. It can be used in many creative ways.

1 Cut out a cactus shape in cardboard. Use a paintbrush to apply PVA glue to the cardboard and use papier mâché pulp to mould the cactus shape on both sides. Smooth the edges off with finger and thumb. Leave to dry.

2 Cut a slit in the lid and insert the cactus. Secure it in place with extra pulp. Make small cone shapes. Dot glue around the edge of the lid and fix them on. Leave to dry.

3 Apply a coat of emulsion paint to the box and lid and leave to dry. If necessary, apply a second coat.

4 Use a paintbrush to apply green poster paints to lid, box and cactus. Decorate cactus and cones with relief paint – this is easy to use and gives a good three-dimensional effect. When dry spray with varnish.

Chequered
tissue

Revamp a cardboard shoe box inexpensively by covering it with colourful tissue papers. Copy the chequered pattern shown here or apply torn tissue shapes such as spots or hearts.

2 Completely cover the lid and box inside and out with the background colour tissue paper. Overlap the strip edges and stick the excess tissue to the underside.

You **will need . . .**

- Shoe box
- Coloured tissue paper
- Ruler
- PVA medium
- Flat paintbrush

1 Use a light-coloured tissue paper for the background. Tear into 1–5cm (⅜–2in) strips. Apply PVA medium to the lid. Apply a strip. Smooth out. Brush with PVA medium.

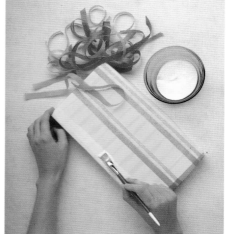

3 Brush a line of PVA medium down the centre of the lid and lay two coloured tissue paper strips side by side. Add another pair of "stripes" equidistant and parallel to the central stripes in the same way.

4 Stick the stripes to the sides of the lid, cut off the excess 1cm (⅜in) beyond the lid edges and stick to the inside. Brush with PVA medium to secure in place.

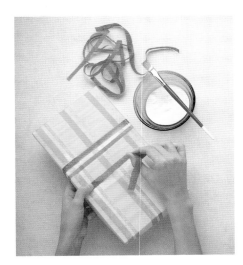

5 Apply pairs of coloured strips at right angles to the stripes to make a plaid pattern. Tear squares of tissue paper and apply to each square of the plaid.

Weaving spells

Strips of painted card are woven into a box and lid. The weave creates an effective broken pattern from the original painted design.

You will need . . .

- Card – up to 1mm thick
- Acrylic paints, various colours
- Paintbrush
- Scissors
- Scalpel
- Blunt knife
- Clear varnish

To prepare the card, measure and mark 32cm (12½in) square on the card. Use a paintbrush and bright acrylic colours to decorate both sides. Allow to dry.

1 To make the lid, cut the card into 16 strips 2cm (¾in) wide. Take 12 of the strips and weave six strips over and under the other six. Tighten the weave so that it leaves a solid square with the ends equal.

2 To make bending the strips easier, use a scalpel to very lightly score around the edge of the woven square. Bend the scored strips upright.

3 To make the sides of the lid, use the remaining four strips. Thread them in and out of the upright strips. Finish the ends in the middle of an inward-facing strip.

4 To finish the upright strips, measure 2cm (¾in) from the base and score. Bend the strips alternately in and out. Measure another 2cm (¾in) and score. Measure 1cm (⅜in) and cut. Bend each one over the side strip. Tuck it in using a blunt knife.

For the base, follow steps 1–4, but cut the strips 1.5cm (⅝in) wide so the base will fit the lid. To make the base deeper, weave in three side strips. Apply varnish to the box and lid.

Child's **elebox**

This brightly coloured box is an easy project to make with children's help. The cardboard elephant on top of the box is for holding pencils and other stationery items.

You **will need . . .**

- Hat or shoe box
- Pencil
- Scissors
- Medium grade sandpaper
- Spray paint/poster paint in green and turquoise
- Brightly coloured paper
- PVA glue
- Paintbrush
- Yellow relief paint
- Paper ribbon or twisted tissue
- Card
- Spray varnish

1 Mark and cut a wavy edge to the lid. Sandpaper rough edges. Paint the lid and box in different colours. Cut or tear coloured paper dots and triangles and glue them to the sides of the lid.

2 Make a simple elephant template. Cut out enough coloured shapes to go round the box, plus two for the lid. Decorate each one with coloured papers. Use relief paint for details.

3 Glue the elephants evenly round the box. Twist tails from paper ribbon. Join them to the trunk of the elephant behind.

4 Mount two elephants on thin card. Cut out. To stick them together: cut four small equal rectangles of card. Fold each into three equal sections. Glue two pieces onto the back of the body. Position the other two pieces on the feet, so that they can be stuck to the lid. Glue them together and upright on the lid.

Alphabet **set**

Dry letter transfer comes in many different scripts, colours and sizes, and makes it possible to create a box such as this very easily.

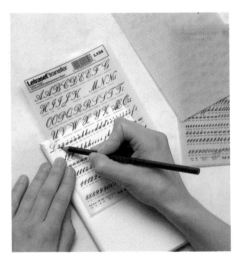

You will need ...

- Wooden box with lid
- White primer paint
- Flat, fine, square-tipped paintbrush
- Fine sandpaper
- White and yellow enamel paint
- Pencil
- Clear varnish
- 4 sheets of dry letter transfer (Letraset black and gold Palace Script was used here)

1 Paint white primer onto the box. Sand down the box until it feels smooth.

2 Using the paintbrush, evenly cover the box with enamel paint. Use white with a dash of yellow. Give the box two coats, sanding down between each one. An even coat is achieved by not loading the brush too fully with paint. Make sure the brushmarks all go the same way.

3 Rub down the dry letter transfer using a pencil on the reverse side. Use the markers on the sheet to keep the spacing even. Carefully paint clear varnish over the box. Dry letter transfer can be quite delicate, so use a fine brush.

Découpage

Découpage is a traditional craft. Paper motifs are cut out and glued to a smooth surface. Many coats of varnish are then applied to give the effect of inlay. As well as printed papers, experiment with fabric, sweet wrappers and even fine metals.

Fabric **découpage**

Fabric is an interesting alternative material to paper for découpage work, especially on woven surfaces such as this bamboo box.

1 Cut open a plastic carrier bag to use as a protective surface. Choose a large motif on the fabric that will fit on the box lid and select smaller ones to fit on the sides. Roughly cut them out. Using a paintbrush, coat the back of the fabric with PVA medium to help prevent fraying. Set aside to dry.

2 Cut out motifs and brush the backs with PVA medium. Stick the large motif on top of the lid, and the smaller motifs to the sides. Leave to dry.

3 Using a paintbrush, apply six coats of polyurethane varnish, allowing each coat to dry before applying the next. The varnish will protect the box and seal the motifs.

1 Using a paintbrush, apply blue emulsion paint to all surfaces of the box. Allow to dry and apply a second coat.

2 Mix the wallpaper paste. Cut the paper lace into short sections to fit the six edges of the lid. Use your fingers to apply the paste to the box edges and to the back of the paper lace. Place each section on the lid and smooth the overlapping areas.

Découpage in flower

You will need . . .

- Hexagonal cardboard box with separate lid
- Blue emulsion paint
- Paintbrush
- Wallpaper paste
- 1 metre (1yd) paper lace
- Small scissors
- Victorian scrap of flowers
- Clear acrylic satin varnish
- Varnish brush

There are many possibilities for the simple technique of découpage to decorate boxes. Here, a Victorian motif is enhanced by the texture of paper lace.

3 Cut out the motif for the centre and use the wallpaper paste to stick in place. Smooth carefully with your fingers and allow to dry.

4 Cut a strip of paper lace in half lengthways and apply with paste. Align the straight edge with the base of the box, and smooth carefully.

5 When dry, apply three coats of acrylic varnish, allowing each coat to dry before applying the next.

Bow-tie box

A simple stylish box to make for Fathers' Day, Christmas or for a birthday present. It's a fun project for children to make. You can vary the decoration endlessly. The finished box is sure to be original and eye catching.

1 Sand the box lid and base with fine sandpaper and paint with black acrylic paint. Cut out bow tie shapes (or make up your own shapes).

2 Paste a light film of découpage glue onto the back of the cut outs. With fingers, smooth the shapes onto the box with your fingers. Smooth out any bubbles and the edges.

3 Using a paintbrush, coat the paper and box lid with découpage glue to give a matt finish. Leave to dry. A second coat can be applied if desired. Brush base of box with glue and leave to dry.

Garden collage

Steel engraved roses on wrapping paper, photocopies of wood engravings from books and colour illustrations of flowers are all used here. Antique and crackle varnishes are used to age the box.

You **will need . . .**

- Selection of illustrations – originals or copies
- Scalpel
- Round box
- Rubber glue (spray glue will wrinkle when varnished)
- Aging or antique varnish
- Paintbrush
- Crackle varnish

1 Select the material and cut out, using a scalpel for fine detail.

2 Arrange the pieces into a collage on the box and glue them into place.

3 Apply aging or antique varnish to darken the material. Follow the crackle varnish manufacturer's instructions to apply the crackle varnish.

World in a box

Reproduction maps are readily obtained from museums and specialist map shops. A terrestial map was used here, but a map of the night sky would also be very effective.

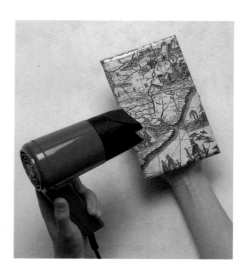

1 Use the ruler and pencil to measure the box and mark out your map to cover it. Cut out. Glue down the map piece ensuring that the edges are neat.

2 If your map is on absorbent paper, give it a coat of clear varnish. Then apply the oil-based aging varnish. Apply the crackle varnish when the aging varnish is almost dry. The surface should be dry enough for your finger to run lightly over it, yet still sticky if you press lightly down.

3 Allow the box to dry in a warm room. Use a hairdryer if cracks have not appeared, but be careful not to overheat the box as this will lift off the crackle layer.

4 Once the surface is dry, rub sepia artist's oil paint into the cracks with a soft cloth. Rub very gently using a circular motion. Using a clean cloth, rub away the excess oil paint. Protect the surface with a coat of clear, oil-based varnish.

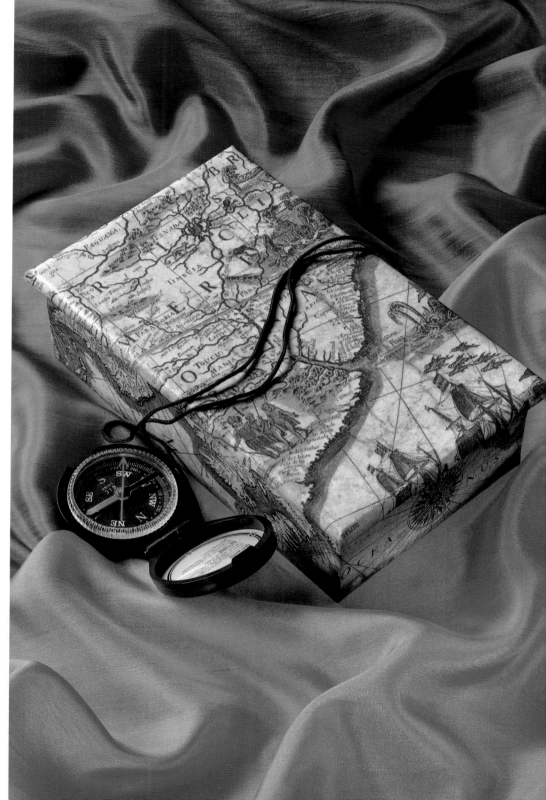

Stamps **galore**

Stamps are ready-made shapes to work with and decorating this box is a good way of using up old ones. Be inventive with the patterns you make.

You **will need . . .**

- Selection of stamps
- Round box
- Antique varnish
- Paintbrush
- Rubber glue (spray glue will wrinkle when varnished)

1 Sort the stamps according to colour. Before applying any glue, experiment with arranging the stamps into a variety of patterns. Arrange a selection into a rosette shape, sticking them lightly together so that other contrasting stamps can be slipped in behind as a background.

2 When you are satisfied with the design, glue the stamps in position on the box. Use a paintbrush to apply an even coat of antique varnish.

3

Paint effects

Nowadays, traditional paint techniques such as tortoiseshell and verdigris are within anyone's reach, while stencilling and stamping are ideal for the nervous painter, as professional results are easy to achieve.

1 Paint an orange border around the sides and ends of the box. Paint an orange panel on the lid, leaving a border. Paint this border and the central panels on the box pink. Allow to dry.

2 Make a simple skeleton template. Lay it on a piece of metal foil, secure with adhesive, and draw around it with a dry ballpoint pen. Draw the parts to be cut away on the template.

Day of the dead

The Mexican Day of the Dead is based on the belief that the dead can visit their old homes without being seen by the living, and recreations of skulls and skeletons play an important role in the festivities.

You **will need . . .**

- Rectangular shaped wooden box with lid
- Acrylic paints in bright orange and bright pink
- Paintbrush
- Skeleton template
- Aluminium foil .004 gauge 60 x 15cm (24 x 6in)
- Adhesive tape
- Dry ballpoint pen
- Small pointed scissors
- Bradawl
- 1cm (⅜in) brass-headed escutcheon pins
- Pin hammer
- Pinking shears

3 Remove the template. Cut out the skeleton shape and the sections in between the "ribs" and "bones". Draw lines to mark the fingers and toes.

4 Centre the skeleton on the lid. Using a bradawl, mark holes through the foil into the metal. Using a pin hammer, tap in escutcheon pins to secure the skeleton to the lid.

5 Cut strips of foil 1cm (⅜in) wide using pinking shears. Use escutcheon pins to secure the strips around the skeleton. In the same way, attach strips on each side of the box as shown.

Lovely **lace**

This pretty giftbox is ideal for presenting a special gift. The delicate filigree effect is created by spray painting through paper doilies. The box is fastened with a double bow of golden ribbons.

You **will need . . .**

- White oval box with separate lid
- Paper doilies
- Scissors
- Spray glue
- Gold spray paint
- Newspapers
- Lighter fuel
- Soft cloth
- Gold wire-edged ribbon

1 Use the lid as a template to cut an oval from the centre of a doily. Applying the glue sparingly, stick it onto the lid. Cut the rest of the doily into sections. Stick these lightly to the sides of the lid. Cut sections from doilies and glue them to the sides of the box.

2 Cover the surrounding area with newspaper when spray painting. Spray the lid with gold paint, applying it in thin coats. Allow the paint to dry between coats. Spray the box gold.

3 When dry, peel off the doilies. To remove any glue, wipe the surface with lighter fuel and a soft cloth. Tie gold ribbon around the box. Slip another length under the knot and fasten in a bow. Cut the tails of the bow in chevrons.

Glitzy kitsch

Glitter paints are great fun to use. This wacky box has bold, glittery floral motifs and sparkling cabouchon jewellery stones.

2 Glue a large jewellery stone in the centre of each flower outline. Glue small stones in the gaps between: these will form the centre of smaller flowers.

You **will need . . .**

- Box
- Glitter paints
- Cabouchon jewellery stones
- Acrylic gesso or emulsion paint
- Thin card
- Craft paint
- All-purpose household glue
- Pencil
- Scissors
- Paintbrush

1 If you have a dark-coloured box, use a paintbrush to apply an undercoat of acrylic gesso or emulsion paint. Leave to dry. Cut out simple flower shapes from thin card to use as templates. Arrange the templates on the box and draw around them.

3 Working on one side of the box at a time, apply glitter paints to fill in the large flower shapes and create petals around the small jewellery stones.

4 Draw stems and leaves with gold glitter paint in between the flowers.

5 Fill in the unpainted areas with silver glitter paint. Leave to dry then touch up any bare areas with more glitter paint.

Tortoiseshell
book box

This smart tortoiseshell effect book box would have pride of place in any library. Fake tortoiseshell was developed in the seventeenth century to meet the demand for the real thing and has remained a very popular paint technique.

1 Use a paintbrush to apply a coat of primer to the outside of the box, the edges of the underside of the "book covers", and a little over the spine of the book. Leave to dry. Apply two coats of yellow gloss paint. Allow to dry. Using a decorator's brush, apply teak varnish to one cover.

2 Use the decorator's brush to mark zig-zags in the varnish, working diagonally from one corner to the other. Dab on large dots of teak varnish at random.

3 Dilute burnt umber and black oil paint with a little white spirit on a tile. With an artist's paintbrush, paint squiggles of burnt umber paint in the same direction as the diagonal zig-zags. Paint smaller squiggles of black paint in the gaps.

4 Apply more teak varnish in the same direction as the zig-zags. Apply another coat at right angles to the previous brushstrokes. Allow to dry. Decorate the other surfaces in the same way.

5 Apply a coat of clear gloss varnish. Set aside to dry. Cut a strip of leatherette paper to the width of the spine plus 1cm (⅜in). Use PVA glue to stick it to the spine, turning the ends over the edges. Cut and stick a rectangle of black leatherette paper to the underside of the cover.

Vintage verdigris

Many metals corrode when the surface comes into contact with the air. Verdigris is the name of the resulting tarnished patination and it can be reproduced easily with paints.

You **will need . . .**

- Metal box with knob or handle
- Masking tape
- Grey metal primer spray paint
- Emulsion paint in pale aquamarine and mid aquamarine
- Viridian designer's gouache
- Fine grade steel wool
- Burnt umber watercolour paint
- Paintbrush
- Polyurethane varnish
- Sprig of artificial ivy

1 Cover the knob or handle with masking tape. Spray the metal primer paint onto the box and lid in a well-ventilated and protected area. Using a paintbrush, apply an undercoat of pale aquamarine emulsion paint to the box and leave to dry.

2 Apply to the box and lid the two shades of aquamarine emulsion paint and the viridian designer's gouache, blending the colours together.

3 Distress the surface by gently rubbing it with wire wool to reveal the undercoat and even the metal in places.

4 Apply a dilute coat of burnt umber watercolour paint to give an aged effect to the box and lid. Allow to dry, then remove the masking tape. Apply two coats of matt varnish to protect the surface. Twist the end of an artificial sprig of ivy around the knob or handle.

Very fishy

Stencilling is a popular way of applying paint as professional results can be achieved so quickly. There is a huge range of stencils.

1 Apply paint thinned with water to the box to show the wood grain. Cut out the stencil using a craft knife on a cutting mat. Fix the stencil to the box lid with masking tape. Apply masking tape around the first areas to be coloured – in this case the fish body – to protect the surrounding cut-outs from paint.

2 Use a flat paintbrush to apply a thin film of paint to a tile or old plate. Holding the stencil brush upright, dab at the paint, taking care not to overload the brush. Apply the paint to the cut-outs by keeping the brush upright and moving it in a circular motion. Allow to dry then peel off the tape from the next cut-outs.

3 Stencil the next colour as before. When the paint is dry stencil the remaining colours. Stencil some of the cut-outs with gold paint to create highlights. Stencil smaller motifs on the sides of the box. To protect the surface, apply three coats of water-based varnish, allowing each coat to dry before applying the next.

Combed paint swirl

The simple technique of running a rubber comb over wet paint creates a striking pattern, enhanced by wavy lines and dots – an ancient and primitive design.

You will need ...

- Round plywood box 18cm (7in) diameter
- Water-based paint (any light colour)
- Paintbrush
- Dark blue water-based paint
- Rubber comb
- Quick drying acrylic varnish
- Varnish brush

1 Using a paintbrush, apply two coats of water-based paint to the box and lid. Allow the first coat to dry before applying the next.

2 Brush the dark blue paint onto the lid. Immediately comb in the fan-shaped pattern. Comb a "flower" in the centre. Apply blue paint on the side of the lid, and comb a wavy line into the paint.

3 Scratch wavy lines and dots in the panels as shown. Repeat on the sides of the box. Allow to dry. Apply three coats of varnish.

Swish fish

This stylish box is made using a template. It is decorated with a stencilled and sponged effect but could simply be spattered with paint.

2 Make the lid in the same way. Line the joints with tissue paper applied with PVA glue.

You **will need . . .**

- Thin cardboard
- Scissors
- Glue gun
- Tissue paper
- PVA glue
- White emulsion paint
- String
- Poster paints in light green, dark green, blue and orange
- Paintbrush
- Toothbrush
- Scalpel
- Small stencil brush
- Matt or spray varnish

Cardboard shapes for the box:
- 1 fish shape
- 2 equal, wide rectangular side pieces
- 1 small, wide and folded rectangle for the tail

For the lid:
- 1 fish shape, as above
- 2 narrow equal side pieces
- 1 narrow, folded tail piece

1 To make the box: use the glue gun to stick the two box side strips to one fish shape. Allow to dry. Glue on the wide tail piece.

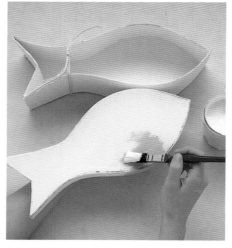

3 Apply a coat of emulsion paint inside and outside of the base and lid. Allow to dry. If necessary, apply a second coat. Before the paint is dry, check that the lid fits. If the base is too wide, tie string round the tail area and leave overnight.

4 Apply light green paint to the box and lid. With a toothbrush, spatter with darker green. When dry, spatter with blue and orange.

5 For further decoration, make simple paper stencils of various shapes. Mix a stiff consistency of both dark and light colours. Apply the light colour using a small stencil brush. Sponge on the darker colour. When dry, apply matt or spray varnish.

Rubber stamp **medley**

A variety of rubber stamps is available from craft shops to purchase. Here, a combination of small linocuts, wooden type and small steel engravings are used.

You **will need . . .**

- Brown paper
- Round wooden box
- Scissors
- Stamps
- Oil-based linoleum inks – various colours
- Linoleum roller
- Wooden spoon
- Rubber glue
- Paintbrush
- Clear varnish

1 On a sheet of brown paper, carefully draw round the lid and cut out. Measure and cut out a long rectangle to exactly cover the sides of the box.

2 Squeeze a blob of oil-based linoleum ink onto a glass slab. Use the roller to distribute the ink evenly on the slab. Using the inked lino roller, ink up the stamps.

3 Place the brown paper on top of an inked stamp. Using a wooden spoon, rub the paper to transfer the ink from the stamp. To finish, use a paintbrush to apply glue to the box, then stick the back of the measured, printed brown paper to it. Coat with clear varnish.

Natural choice

*The country is an
endless source of
inspiration for
decorating with natural
materials. Always be
considerate of the
environment. Collect
only fallen leaves and
flowers unless they are
in your own garden.
Craft shops and other
specialist shops supply
dried flowers, colourful
feathers and shells.*

Fragrance of lavender

A delicate aroma of lavender from this pretty box will scent its surroundings. For a more intense fragrance, fill the box with potpourri and leave the lid ajar.

You **will need . . .**

- Coloured wicker box
- Thick string or jute
- All-purpose household glue
- Scissors
- Lavender sprigs

1 Dab some glue onto one end of the string to prevent it from unravelling. When dry, cut diagonally across the glued end.

2 Coil the string closely into a spiral and glue to one front corner of the lid. Arrange the string around the edge in a wavy pattern, with loops. Glue in place and cut off the excess string. Decorate the sides in the same way.

3 Arrange sprigs of lavender on the lid. Trim the ends if necessary, then apply glue to the lid and secure the flowers in position.

Beaded raffia box

The random method of weaving coloured raffia on this funky mesh hat box can be applied to any woven box. Shiny beads threaded onto the raffia add an interesting change of texture.

You **will need . . .**

- Woven box
- Coloured raffia
- Large-eyed needle
- Scissors
- Beads with large holes

1 Bunch together raffia in separate colours. Twist the lengths together. Wrap the twisted raffia around the lid rim and tie in a knot. Trim the trailing ends with scissors.

2 Thread a single length of raffia onto a needle. Fasten the end to the rim. Sew the twisted raffia to the rim with long diagonal stitches, threading on beads as you work.

3 Thread another single length of raffia. Thread it in and out of the mesh, threading a bead on each stitch. Tie the ends of the raffia to the mesh. Weave different coloured raffia in rows around the box. Leave space at the top for the lid.

1 Apply a 1.5cm (½in) band of glue around the base of the box. Wind string tautly round the box, pushing it into position. Repeat until you reach the top.

2 To make a round decoration, cut an 18cm (7in) length of string, apply glue sparingly along its length and wind into a spiral. Glue the decorations evenly around the base.

String **thing**

String is easy to work with and the decoration can be simple or complex. Coloured string is readily available and contrasts well with natural colours. Incorporate bands of contrasting colour for extra flair.

You will need . . .

- Wooden or cardboard box with lid
- PVA glue
- Paintbrush
- String in 3 colours
- Scissors
- Pencil
- Card

3 To make the top tassel, wrap coloured string round a 6.5cm (2½in) wide piece of card 20 times and cut. Wrap string in a contrasting colour round the card 40 times and cut.

4 Carefully remove the string from the card. Wind a small amount of string near the base and secure with a knot. Cut the folded ends to form a tassel and glue it to the centre of the lid.

5 To make the front decoration, cut several 10cm (4in) lengths of string and secure with string round the middle, tied with a knot. Apply with PVA glue and stick it onto the contrasting string band.

Shell box

Bright blue conjures up the sea and sky on a sunny day. Shells complement this idea and are used as feet for the box, attached to it with paper stuffing.

You **will need . . .**

- Rectangular box with lid
- Blue acrylic paint
- Paintbrush
- Shells in different sizes and colours
- PVA glue
- China glue

1 Using a paintbrush, coat the box with bright blue paint. Stuff paper into four big shells to use as feet for the box.

2 Apply PVA glue to the paper. Stick one to each corner of the box, matching the centre point of the shells with the corners. Use China glue to stick shells onto the rim of the lid.

3 In the same way, stick more shells onto the centre of the lid. Arrange the remaining shells in a pleasing design and glue in place.

Seaside
treasure

Put holiday souvenirs to good use by decorating a straw box with seaside finds to evoke memories of happy excursions.

You **will need . . .**

- Straw box
- Broken fishing net
- Scissors
- Driftwood
- Seagull feathers
- Selection of shells including a crab shell
- Glue gun or all-purpose household glue

1 Cut a section from a broken fishing net. Bunch it up and glue to the centre of the lid. An old netted shopping bag could be used instead. Poke driftwood into the netting, pointing toward the corners. Glue in place.

2 Glue a large shell and crab shell on top of the netting or two large shells if you do not have a crab shell.

3 Glue more shells into the netting and to the driftwood. Glue small shells to the lid. Glue small shells at random to the lid edges and box sides.

Spice is nice

This aromatic container is covered with spices and dried fruit slices. The cinnamon is trimmed in two different lengths to fit neatly.

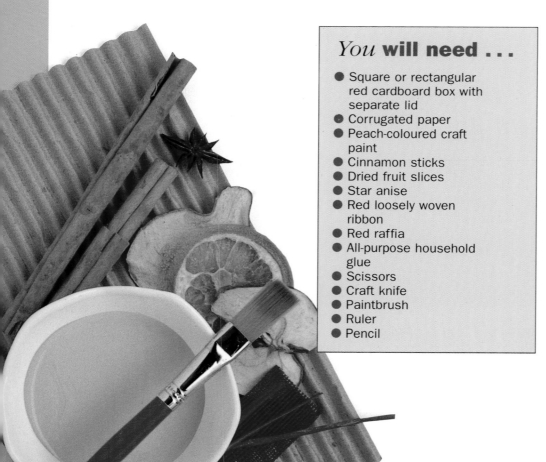

You will need . . .

- Square or rectangular red cardboard box with separate lid
- Corrugated paper
- Peach-coloured craft paint
- Cinnamon sticks
- Dried fruit slices
- Star anise
- Red loosely woven ribbon
- Red raffia
- All-purpose household glue
- Scissors
- Craft knife
- Paintbrush
- Ruler
- Pencil

1 Using a paintbrush, paint the box with peach-coloured craft paint, diluted with water so the red box colour shows through. Measure and cut a piece of corrugated paper to fit the lid. Apply household glue and stick in place.

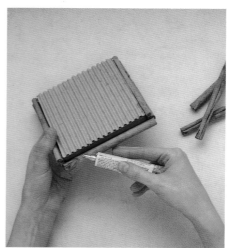

2 Cut cinnamon sticks for the edges of the lid. Glue them in pairs to opposite edges, then to the remaining sides, as shown.

3 Using a dab of glue, attach the ends of two lengths of ribbon to the underside of the lid on opposite sides and tie a knot on top. Trim the ends of the ribbon diagonally.

4 Pierce the dried fruits and thread with raffia. Slip the raffia under the ribbon knot tying it around three more short cinnamon sticks. Trim the ends and glue on a star anise.

Punch-work
box

The wooden box with tin lid used here is readily available from shops or department stores. Keep your design simple for full effect.

You **will need . . .**

- ● Wooden box with tin lid (biscuit tin)
- ● Masking tape
- ● Bradawl
- ● Paper
- ● Pencil

1 Draw the design on paper. Use masking tape to secure it to the lid. Following the pattern, punch equally spaced holes with a bradawl through the paper into the metal. If the lid is thick metal, do the punching over the box. If it is thinner metal, punch onto a piece of softwood.

2 Work on the star and circles first, then punch the eight-pointed stars at each corner and in the centre of the lid.

3 When the design is complete, peel off the paper to reveal the punched pattern.

Autumn leaves

A purchased recycled box with simple raffia decoration on the base was used for this project, but a plain shoe box is equally suitable. Pressed leaves are a colourful and cheap decorative material.

1 Leaves can be pressed at any time of the year but the rich colours of autumn make the best selection. Lay the leaves between sheets of newsprint, weigh down with books and leave for three to four weeks. Smooth out leaves with a light iron on a medium heat.

2 Select some leaves in contrasting colours. Arrange them on the lid of the box, balancing the colours and overlapping some of the leaves. Use a paintbrush to apply glue to the underside of each leaf and press firmly into position. Leave to dry.

3 Use a paintbrush to apply a coat of acrylic matt varnish for a natural look. Apply a spray varnish for a shiny finish.

Feather pompom

The "distressed" treatment of the paint creates an antique effect and the feathers introduce an unusual three-dimensional aspect to the box surface.

1 Apply gold paint to the box. When dry, apply the grey colour over the gold and allow to dry. Rub the surface with sandpaper to reveal some of the gold colour and achieve a speckled, antique effect.

2 Use a paintbrush to dot glue on the box. Attach each feather to the box by its base, so that they overlap. Repeat the process on the rim of the lid.

3 The pompom: fold the ribbon double lengthways. Attach the feathers to it with loose stitches. Use the stitched yarn to draw the ribbon together to create the pompom. Secure with a knot. Glue it to the lid.

Pressed flower bouquet

Pressed flowers on a gold background give this box a delicate richness. Make your own choice of flowers – White September and Chrysanthemum are used here.

You **will need . . .**

- Round wooden box
- White undercoat paint
- Paintbrush
- Gold powder
- Soft cloth
- Flowers of your choice
- Blotting paper
- Flower press
- Rubber glue
- Clear gloss varnish

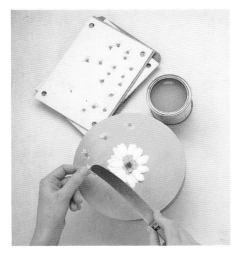

1 Using a paintbrush, apply white undercoat to the wooden box and lid. Allow to dry. Apply gold powder using a soft cloth, rubbing in small circles into the wood grain.

2 Pinch off the stems from the flowers. Arrange them between sheets of blotting paper and place in a flower press. Secure the screws tightly. Leave the flowers in the press for a fortnight, or longer if the flowers are large.

3 Carefully remove the flowers from the press and arrange them on the lid. Apply glue to the lid and adhere the flowers. When dry, using a paintbrush, apply a coat of clear gloss varnish.

Fabulous fabric

From traditional boxes incorporating age-old sewing skills such as quilting to no-sew projects for the reluctant needleworker, this chapter presents a delightfully eclectic choice of boxes using a wide selection of fabrics and techniques.

Quilted **casket**

*Design your own pattern to quilt by hand –
a plain running stitch secures the three
layers. The combination of velvet, taffeta
and quilting creates a taste of luxury.*

You **will need . . .**

- Oval or round shaped box with separate lid
- Dark red velvet 15 x 12cm (6 x 5in)
- Lining material (cotton) 15 x 12cm (6 x 5in)
- Filling material (cotton wool or synthetic cotton wool) 15 x 12cm (6 x 5in)
- Chalk
- Dark red sewing yarn
- PVA glue
- Dark red taffeta 20 x 15cm (8 x 6in)
- Dark red string

1 Use the lid as a template to cut out pieces of velvet, lining and filling material, plus 2cm (¾in) allowance. Using chalk trimmed to a thin point, mark a simple pattern of quilting lines.

2 Pin together the velvet (with right side on top), filling material and lining. Sew plain running stitches along the marked pattern lines. Seal the quilt edges with glue.

3 Glue the taffeta to the rim of the lid. Apply glue to the top of the lid and attach the quilt securely.

4 For a clean, decorative finish, twist dark red string and pin it on the velvet around the rim. Stitch in place. Seal the edges of the taffeta with glue. Apply glue around the base of the box and stick on the taffeta.

Sea **chest**

Silk moistened with water and glue is very soft and easy to form. Here it is manipulated to create a wave-like effect.

2 Cut the silk fabric in half. Moisten it with water. Using a paintbrush, cover the moist fabric with glue.

You **will need . . .**

- Square or rectangular box with lid
- Blue acrylic paint
- Paintbrush
- Enough white silk organza to cover box and lid
- PVA glue
- Glass pearls in different sizes, transparent and blue
- China glue

1 Paint the box and lid bright blue. Allow to dry.

3 Wind the glued fabric round the box, moulding it into wave shapes as you go. Repeat steps 2 and 3 for the lid.

4 When the fabric is dry, glue the pearls over the box and lid in an irregular design. Aim for a natural and organic effect.

5 Using china glue, stick transparent glass pearls as feet at each corner of the base of the box. Allow to dry thoroughly before standing the box upright.

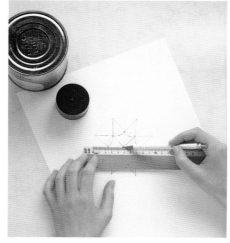

1 Place the lid on paper and draw round it. Find a smaller circular object, place it in the centre of the first circle and draw round it. Find the centre point, divide into equal parts and design the star.

2 Cut out the separate segments. Place each one onto the fabric and draw round it, adding a 5mm (⅛in) allowance. Cut out the shapes.

"French star" **patchwork**

Design your own pattern to recreate in patchwork. No sewing is involved – glue is used to secure the pieces. There are plenty of inexpensive books on patchwork full of other designs you could use.

You **will need . . .**

- Round box with lid
- Paper
- Pencil
- Ruler
- Small, sharp scissors
- Fabric pieces
- Paintbrush
- PVA glue
- Gold string

3 Apply PVA glue to the paper pattern segments. Fold the fabric edges over the paper shapes.

4 Snip the corners and trim the edges so the pieces lie flat. Use a paintbrush to apply glue to each piece. Stick the pieces to the lid, forming the design.

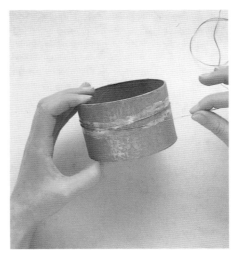

5 Apply glue to the side of the box and wind the gold string around it.

Pin-up in silk

This pretty gilded box decorated with silk and beads makes a perfect present for someone who does embroidery. Sawdust can be substituted for wadding for a traditionally filled pin cushion.

You **will need . . .**

- Wooden heart-shaped box with lid
- Sealer
- Metallic powders in gold and bronze
- Metallic paint medium
- Cardboard
- Scissors
- Wadding
- Silk
- PVA glue
- Paintbrush
- Paper for stencil
- Stencil brush
- Dressmaker's pins
- Gold and pearl beads
- "Gold" charm

2 Make a card template using the lid. Cut a heart from the wadding. Cut a silk heart 13mm (½in) larger. Put them together with the card on top. Glue the edge of the card and turn the silk over it.

1 Cover the box with sealer and allow to dry. Mix gold powder with the metallic medium. Apply with light brushstrokes, a little at a time. Allow to dry. Apply touches of the bronze colour.

3 Cut out a smaller heart stencil and centre it over the silk heart. Mix gold powder with metallic paint medium and lightly stencil the heart shape. Leave to dry.

4 Pin pearl beads around the gold heart, and the gold charm in the centre. Pin pearl and gold beads around the outside edge.

5 Apply a thin layer of PVA glue to the cardboard backing and place in the centre of the gilded lid and press firmly. Leave to dry.

You **will need . . .**

- Oval box with lid
- Medium-weight wadding
- Latex glue
- Red and green slub fabric
- Dressmaking pins
- Needlework scissors
- Thin card
- Purple wire-edged ribbon 4cm (1½in) wide
- Pink ribbon 1.5cm (⅝in) wide
- Pink ribbon the width of the side of the lid
- Needle and thread
- Gold coin pendants
- Beads
- Large gold pendant

Echoes of Asia

This luxurious fabric-covered box is influenced by the rich colours of Asia. Gold coins and a glorious elephant motif complete the theme.

1 Cut an oval of wadding to fit the lid and an oval of red fabric with a margin of 2cm (¾in) added. Glue the wadding to the lid. Pin the fabric centrally on the wadding. Glue the raw edges to the sides of the lid, snipping the fabric so that it lies flat.

2 Cut a strip of green fabric to fit round the box plus 2.5cm (1in). Glue one end in place. Wrap the strip around the box. Turn under the other end and glue sparingly. Glue the excess fabric to the base. Glue the fabric inside the top of the box.

3 Cut an oval of thin card 3mm (⅛in) smaller than the box base. Cover it with green fabric and glue it to the base inside the box. Glue narrow pink ribbon over the raw edges inside the box.

4 Pleat the purple ribbon. Make a small cut on each side. Knot a short length of ribbon at this point. Sew on a gold coin and a bead to the ends. Glue the loose ends inside the lid.

5 For the edge of the lid: sew a row of gold coins and beads to the pink ribbon. Glue it around the sides, finishing it neatly. Open the ribbon loops on top of the box. Sew a large gold pendant and a bead to the front of the box.

Tasselled **tapestry**

The sumptuous choice of fabric used to cover this box gives it a very regal look. The box is lined with a coordinating fabric and a chunky tasselled cord adds a final touch of grandeur.

1 To cover the lid: cut enough tapestry fabric to cover the whole lid plus 1cm (⅜in) along each edge. Apply latex glue to the top and long sides of the lid. Stick the fabric to the lid. Fold under the fabric at the short sides, a neat fold at each corner. Mark the foldlines with pins.

2 Open out the fabric. Cut away the excess to within 1.5cm (⅝in) of the pins. Cut the fabric level with the edge of the lid. Refold and glue in place.

3 To make a lining for the lid: cut a strip of slub fabric measuring the total length of all the sides plus 12cm (4¾in). Its width measures the lid depth plus 2cm (¾in). At 2cm (¾in) from one end of the strip, pin a pleat 1cm (⅜in) deep.

4 To glue the lining to the lid: apply glue to the inside edge of the top of the lid. With the pleat at one corner, stick one edge of the strip to the lid, laying it flat against the side. Continue to apply the strip, pleating it at each corner. Fold the end under. Glue in place.

6 Box lining: cut a strip of slub to cover the sides plus 2cm (¾in) all round. Follow step 4, omitting pleats. Glue the inside edges of the box. Press the fabric flat inside. Trim level. Cover the outside with slub, as in steps 1 and 2. Glue the raw edge inside the box.

5 Pin the raw edge of the lining over the edge of the lid. Snip the corners so the fabric lies flat. Glue in place, leaving the edge raw.

7 To trim: glue lengths of braid over the raw fabric edges on both box and lid. Cover two rectangles of card with slub. Turn the fabric under 1cm (⅜in) and glue. Glue the pieces inside the box and lid. Fasten with the tasselled cord.

Woolly **box**

Wool is a wonderfully textural material.
Try fur fabric as a variation.

1 Paint the box and lid orange. Allow to dry. Stick the wool fibre onto it.

2 Brush diluted PVA glue round the edges of the box to ensure a neat finish. Repeat on the lid.

1 Cut enough felt motifs and contrasting details to decorate the lid and box sides. Cut out a zig-zag design for the lid rim. Sew the details to the main felt shapes with single stitches. Highlight with random stitches.

Felt **good**

Stylized motifs cut from felt are sewn together with vibrant embroidery threads to trim this colourful box. A chunky bead is attached to the top as a practical knob to lift the lid.

You **will need . . .**

- Coloured cardboard box with separate lid
- Coloured felt
- Embroidery scissors
- Stranded cotton embroidery thread
- Sewing needle
- Latex glue
- Heart-shaped beads
- Button
- Bead 2.5cm (1in) in diameter
- Bead 6mm (¼in) in diameter

2 Glue the motifs and zig-zags to the lid and box. Apply the glue sparingly so that it does not seep through the fabric. Sew a heart-shaped bead at each corner of the lid. Fasten the thread ends inside.

3 To attach the knob: thread the needle through the button then through the lid. Thread on the large bead, a heart-shaped bead and the small bead. Insert the needle back through the beads, the lid and out through the other button hole.

4 Tighten the thread so that the beads sit one on top of each other. The button will act as a washer. Knot the thread ends securely together on the button.

6

Design in 3-D

Three-dimensional decorations are an ideal way to revamp an otherwise unusable box. A totally new look can be given to a box just by sticking on a pretty ornament – or you can go to the other extreme and create extravagant sculptural effects by building up the boxes with clay or salt dough.

Cake-deco **container**

Transform a plain box into this elegant classical building with the simple addition of a pair of cake-decorating columns and architectural details cut from mounting board.

2 Glue the smaller pieces of card on top and underneath the lid, in the centre. Weight the lid with heavy books while the glue dries.

You **will need . . .**

- Lidless box, at least 13.5cm (5⅜in) high
- Two cake-decorating columns, each 7.5cm (3in) high
- Mounting board (8-sheet thickness)
- Silver spray paint
- Pencil
- Craft knife
- Ruler
- Heavy books
- All-purpose household glue
- Paintbrush

1 To make the lid: on the mounting board lightly draw round the box base. Add 5mm (¼in) on all sides. Cut out using a ruler and craft knife. Cut two more pieces of mounting board, 1cm (⅜in) smaller on all sides.

3 Glue the columns to the box 4.5cm (1¾in) apart. Cut mounting board 11.5 × 4cm (4½ × 1½in). Cut a triangle: base 12.5cm (5in) long, sides 4cm (1½in) high. Glue them together on the long edges at right angles (90°).

4 Cut two equal triangles: bases 10.5cm (4⅛in), sides 3.5cm (1⅜in). Attach one triangle to the architrave as shown, for extra support. Glue the remaining triangle to the front.

5 Glue the architrave on top of the pillars. Cut two simple window shapes and glue them to the box sides. Spray silver paint over the box and lid inside and out.

Salt dough sweetheart

Salt dough is a traditional folk craft. The dough is modelled and then baked slowly in a domestic oven. This box is studded with twinkling glass jewellery stones and painted with pearlized paints.

2 Arrange small jewellery stones around the edges of the heart. Position a larger stone in the centre. Embed the stones in the dough with the tip of a knife.

You **will need . . .**

- 6 tbsp plain flour
- 3 tbsp salt
- 3 tbsp water
- Bowl
- Airtight container
- Rolling pin
- Baking parchment
- Heart-shaped box
- Small knife
- Glass stones
- Fine sandpaper
- Wood glue
- Pearlized paints
- Paintbrushes
- Yacht varnish

To make the salt dough, mix the flour, salt and half the water. Add the rest of the water, kneading the mixture into a pliable dough. Knead for another five minutes. Set aside in an airtight container for half an hour.

1 Roll out the dough 1cm (⅜in) thick on baking parchment. Using the box lid as a template, cut out a heart. Smooth the edge with a wet finger.

3 Roll 10 balls of dough 1cm (⅜in) in diameter and flatten each slightly. Bake all the dough pieces in an oven at 250°F (120°C/Gas mark ½) for 6½ hours until the dough is completely hard. Turn off the heat and allow the pieces to cool in the oven.

4 Use sandpaper to smooth the edges and underside of the heart. Stick the heart to the lid and the balls to the rim with wood glue. Using a paintbrush, apply turquoise pearlized paint to the lid and box. Leave to dry.

5 Paint details in contrasting colours of pearlized paint using a fine paintbrush. Apply six coats of yacht varnish to the lid, allowing each coat to dry before applying the next, to protect the salt dough. Note: It is important to keep salt dough away from moisture.

Golden **finds**

Densely embellished with exquisite buttons, jewels, and baubles, this must be the ultimate jewelry box.

1 To make the handle, bend an ornate teaspoon into a suitable curved shape. You may need to secure one end of a metal spoon in a vise to bend it. The spoon here is a souvenir from a museum gift shop; it is made of plastic and therefore easy to bend. Glue a string of pearls around the lid circumference.

2 Arrange the materials on the lid in a pleasing design and glue them in place.

3 Fill in the areas between the decorations with gold puff paint and set aside to dry. Decorate the box and sides of the lid to match. Brush the box interior with mother-of-pearl acrylic paint.

Mosaic **magic**

This colourful box is created using the ancient art of mosaics. Broken china and tiles are applied in a random, crazy-paved style around a central chunky ceramic knob.

1 Wrap the china and ceramic tiles in an old towel. Strike with a hammer to break into small pieces.

2 Stick a ceramic cupboard knob to the centre of the lid with tile adhesive. Arrange the mosaic pieces on the lid in a random crazy-paving pattern, leaving a gap of about 3mm (⅛in) between the pieces.

3 Apply tile adhesive, and cover the lid rim and box sides with mosaics. Allow a margin at the top of the box to fit the lid and a border of 5mm (¼in) for the grout. Wipe away excess adhesive. Leave to dry.

4 Spread grout over the ceramic pieces, filling the gaps. Wipe away excess grout with a damp cloth as you work. When the grout is dry, polish with a soft cloth.

Also **astrology**

Horoscopes hold a fascination for many people. This box, decorated with astrological symbols, has a star sign motif modelled from clay on the lid.

You **will need . . .**

- Rectangular box with lid
- Air-drying clay
- Wooden cutting board
- Rolling pin
- Small pointed knife
- Super glue
- Acrylic gesso or emulsion paint
- Indian inks
- Paintbrushes
- Polyurethane matt varnish

1 Roll the clay out flat 6mm (¼in) thick on a wooden cutting board. Use the lid to cut a rectangle. Cut away the centre, leaving a frame. Moisten the knife tip and pat the cut edges to neaten it. Divide the frame into "tiles" by indenting the clay.

2 Model a simple astrological motif from clay to fit within the frame. This water vessel represents Aquarius. Indent details with the knife tip. Set the clay pieces aside to harden overnight.

3 Glue the clay pieces to the box lid. Undercoat the box and lid with acrylic gesso or emulsion paint.

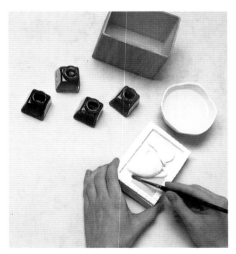

4 Paint the lid and box with Indian inks diluted with water. Paint astrological symbols on the box and sides of the lid. Apply two coats of varnish.

Celestial
star

This heavenly container would make a delightful gift box for a special present. The silver-lined clouds are simple to apply using a natural sponge.

You **will need . . .**

- Star-shaped box
- Acrylic gesso or emulsion paint
- Flat paintbrush
- Blue, white, silver and gold craft paints
- Small natural sponge
- Tile or old plate
- Ornamental cherub
- Super glue

1 Using a paintbrush, apply an undercoat to the box and lid inside and out using acrylic gesso or emulsion paint. When dry, paint with blue craft paint. Apply a thin film of white paint to a tile or old plate. Dab at the paint with a small, damp natural sponge. Dab the sponge lightly onto the lid to suggest clouds.

2 When the "clouds" are dry apply a thin film of silver paint to the tile or plate and dab with the clean, damp sponge. Dab the silver on the lower edge of the clouds. Leave to dry and repeat with gold paint.

3 Glue an ornamental cherub to the top of the lid.

1 Paint the lid and box blue. Paint the inside green. Lightly dab at the green paint with a toothbrush, then run a finger through the bristles to spatter the lid and box with paint. Leave to dry.

Fruity
beauty

Exotic fruits modelled from coloured polymer clay are stuck in bas relief style to this quirky box. Experiment with making other fruits or even vegetables to stick to a practical kitchen storage box.

2 Draw around the lid on baking parchment. Roll a ball of orange clay 4.5cm (1¾in) in diameter. Mould to an oval for the pineapple. Flatten it slightly and place it on the parchment oval to size and position the design. Indent a criss-cross design with the knife tip.

3 Roll green clay out flat 3mm (⅛in) thick. Cut pointed leaf shapes and position them, bending the leaf tips forward. Press the base of the leaves against the pineapple.

4 Roll balls of orange and yellow clay for the citrus fruits. Mould the yellow clay to form the lemons. Cut all the pieces in half, the lemons lengthwise. Reshape the fruits with your fingers. Bake, following the manufacturer's instructions. Allow to cool. Glue the pineapple to the lid and the fruits to the rim. Varnish.

Copper **repoussé**

The repoussé effect on this copper box is made by drawing with a dry ballpoint pen. Work on a soft surface for the marks to indent and create the relief.

You **will need . . .**

- Copper foil .004 gauge
- Ruler
- Dry ballpoint pen
- Strong scissors
- Small pointed scissors
- Double-sided tape
- Short length soft
  copper wire

1 Mark the pattern of the box on the foil using a dry ballpoint pen and ruler. Use strong scissors to cut out the shape and small scissors to snip the fold-over tabs.

2 Lay the foil on a soft surface such as a magazine. Use a dry ballpoint pen and ruler to draw tramlines inside the panels of the box. Draw criss-cross lines within each panel, and stars in the centre of each diamond shape. Add dots into the tramlines.

3 Lay the tape onto the edge of each side. Fold along the scored lines and draw each side up from the base. Fold the lining and tab over the decorated side. Press gently. Before folding the last side over, slip the copper wire into the fold, leaving 3cm (1¼in) at each end.

4 Mark the pattern for the lid slightly larger than the box and allow an extra 1cm (²⁄₅in) all round.

5 Line the reverse of the lid, turning over the edges to secure it. Insert the wire into the folded over section of the lid and twist the wire to join. To secure the hinge, fold the last edge over on the base of the box.

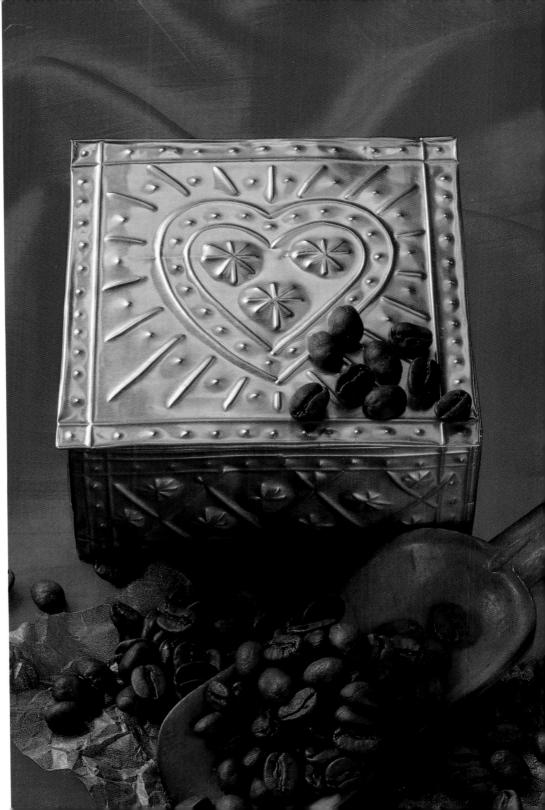

Delicious box

This appetizing confection is actually a round box with a clay "cream cake" modelled over the original lid. The box is deceptively simple to create and the technique can be adapted to make all kinds of favourite pastries.

2 Squeeze a piece of baking foil into a dome. Glue it to the lid. Roll a sausage of clay 1.5 cm (⅝in) thick. Slightly flatten it and wrap it around the lid.

You **will need . . .**

- Round box with separate lid
- Fine corrugated card
- All-purpose household glue
- Pink and white craft paints
- Paintbrushes
- Baking foil
- Wooden cutting board
- Air-drying clay
- Craft knife
- Brown acrylic paint
- Red nail varnish
- Relief paints

1 Cut a strip of corrugated card long enough to wrap around the box, and to the height of the box with the lid on. Glue the strip around the box, level with the base. Paint the box pink.

3 Roll a ball of clay and flatten it between your fingers to a circle 6mm (¼in) thick for the icing. Place the icing over the foil and press onto the pastry. Smooth over the surface of the icing with moistened fingers.

4 Roll a 2cm (¾in) diameter ball of clay for a cherry. Make a dent in it with a paintbrush. Make a depression in the top of the icing. Press in the cherry.

5 Set the clay cake aside to harden. Pull out the original lid. Dilute brown acrylic paint and paint the pastry. Paint the icing white, and the cherry with nail varnish. Dot relief paint on the icing.

Eggstrordinary **fabergé**

This simple egg requires very little skill, it looks ornate but is easy to make. The cardboard egg boxes can be bought at Easter time from toy shops, stationers or gift shops. There is a vast array of beads and sequins available.

You **will need . . .**

- Cardboard Easter egg
- Enamelled silver spray
- Paper fasteners
- Selection of gold and coloured glass beads, leaves etc
- Jewellery glue
- Gold jewellery wire
- Sharp nails or scissors

1 Spray the cardboard egg inside and out with silver enamel spray. Leave to dry. Make an incision with a sharp point at both ends of the egg and on the sides. Insert the paper fasteners.

2 Glue the leaves around the rim. Decorate the paper fasteners with beads, using glue to secure them. Glue four small beads onto the base of the box to allow it to stand upright.

3 Cut three pieces of wire, one the length of the egg and two double the length. Fold in half. Decorate with pearls and beads. Twist the wire pieces around each other.

4 Secure two wires across the egg using the paper fasteners. Finish with the longer piece from one end of the egg to the other. Decorate the top with threaded beads and leaves. The base is decorated with twisted wire fastened onto paper fasteners at each end.

Glossary

This comprehensive list of definitions is useful to refer to if you come across unfamiliar terms in the projects.

Acrylic gesso
A thick, creamy substance that is used as an undercoat, often under gilding. Gesso can be bought at art shops.

Acrylic matt medium
This versatile medium can be used as a varnish, or mixed with gold powder to brush onto a wooden surface.

Acrylic paint
A popular artist's paint that is water soluble when wet but water resistant when dry. Available in a wide range of colours from art shops, the paint dries quickly to a matt finish.

Air-drying clay
A self-hardening modelling clay that dries upon contact with the air. Keep the clay in an airtight container when not in use and moisten with water while you are modelling it.

Antique varnish
Also called ageing varnish. This tinted medium can be brushed onto a decorated box to subtly darken the surface. Refer to the manufacturer's instructions for cleaning brushes and drying times.

Bradawl
A woodworking tool with a metal point that is used to make holes.

Cabouchon jewellery stones
Coloured glass jewellery stones with flat backs for gluing.

Copper foil
Fine gauge metal that can be cut with scissors (use an old pair as the metal will blunt the blades). The foil is thin enough to be folded and embossed.

Crackle varnish
A preparation that gives a cracked, transparent effect. This is achieved by applying a quick-drying medium over a slow-drying one causing cracks to appear in the top layer. Emphasize the cracks by rubbing in oil paint.

Craft knife
A craft knife or scalpel is indispensable for craftwork. Use on a cutting mat to cut smoothly through paper and card. Replace the blades often. do not attempt to cut right through thick card or mounting board at the first approach, instead cut several times gradually deeper and deeper.

Craft paint
A non-toxic quick-drying paint that is usually acrylic based. Craft paints are available at art and craft shops in a large range of colours and finishes include pearl, metallic, matt and glossy.

Cutting mat
A plastic mat available at art shops and large stationers. Use a cutting mat when cutting with a craft knife or scalpel, the surface is self-healing so can be used again and again and is slower to blunt blades than other surfaces.

Designer's gouache
A water-based tube paint that is water-soluble when dry. Gouache is thicker and more opaque than watercolour or acrylic paint.

Emulsion paint
Opaque water-based household paint that can also be used as an undercoat for many other paint finishes.

Escutcheon pins
Fine brass pins that will not split wood when hammered in.

Glitter paint
Colourful plastic particles are suspended in a glue that dries transparent so only the glitter is visible. Glitter paint can be brushed on but is usually squeezed from a tube through a fine nozzle.

Gold powder
Metallic powder made from finely powdered bronze that can be applied with a finger or cloth, or mixed with a medium and brushed on.

Indian inks
Available in small jars from art shops, Indian inks can be thinned with water and applied as a wash.

Linoleum roller
A small roller to roll over rubber stamps or découpaged papers to ensure even coverage.

Masking tape
A low-tack tape that is useful for sticking motifs temporarily in place when arranging them. Always use a very low-tack masking tape and check that it will not mark or tear your material before use.

Mounting board
Thick card made of layers of paper. Available at art and picture-framing shops in various thicknesses. Mounting board is traditionally used to make surrounds or mounts for pictures but is useful for making shapes to add to boxes.

Oil paints
Artist's oil paints are available in tubes from art shops and can be thinned with white spirit. The paints are slow-drying and brushes must be cleaned with white spirit.

Paper ribbon
Often used in giftwrapping and flower-arranging, paper ribbon is a strip of randomly creased paper that comes in the form of a twisted rope.

Plastic putty
A soft putty-like substance that will not harden. It will adhere to most surfaces, so it can be used to hold decorations temporarily in place while you are arranging them.

Polymer clay
A popular modelling material that can be bought at art, craft and toy shops. The clay comes in a range of colours that can be blended together, always wash your hands between colours. The clay is baked in a domestic oven and can be varnished afterwards.

Primer
This term describes any substance that is applied to a surface in preparation for painting. Always use a primer suitable for the type of paint you are using.

PVA medium
PVA stands for polyvinyl acetate. This multi-purpose glue is white when wet and transparent when dry. PVA medium has been used for many of the projects in this book. It can be thinned with water and used as an adhesive and for making papier mâché.

Relief paint
A thick, creamy paint that comes in a tube or bottle with a fine nozzle to distribute the paint and dries standing proud of the surface.

Salt dough
A modelling material made from plain flour, salt and water. Salt dough is baked slowly in a cool oven to harden it. The finished model must have many coats of varnish applied and be kept in a dry atmosphere.

Sealant
A solution painted onto a surface to prevent it affecting the decoration that is applied to it. Sanding sealer is a versatile sealer which can be used on wooden boxes and applied to thin papers to prepare them for découpage.

Stencil board
A hardwearing waxed card used to make stencils.

Stencil brush
This brush has short, thick bristles. Hold the brush upright when stencilling and move in a circular motion to distribute the paint.

Varnish
It is advisable to varnish most completed boxes for protection. Choose a varnish suited to the finish of the box. Water and acrylic based varnishes dry quickly to a clear finish. Polyurethane varnishes are slower to dry and will slightly yellow the surface but are very hardwearing. Always varnish in a dust-free area and use a good quality flat brush, ideally a badger-hair varnishing brush. Clean brushes immediately after use.

Index

Cheryl Owen designed and made:
Safari stripes, Checkered tissue, Fabric découpage, Glitzy kitsch, Very fishy,
Seaside treasure, Celestial star, Golden finds, Fragrance of lavender, Salt-dough sweetheart,
Mosaic magic, Marquetry magic, Tortoiseshell book box, Vintage verdigris,
Tasseled tapestry, Cake-deco container, Spice is nice, Also astrology, Fruity beauty,
Felt good, Delicious box, Lovely lace, Beaded raffia box, Echoes of Asia.

Carol Wilhide designed and made:
Pressed flower bouquet, Rubber stamp medley, Garden collage, Stamps galore,
Weaving spells, World in a box, Alphabet set.

Daniela Zimmermann designed and made:
Sea chest, Shell box, "French star" patchwork, Feather pompom, Quilted casket,
Wooly box.

Deborah Schneebeli-Morrell designed and made:
Day of the dead, Punched-work box, Combed paint swirl, Découpage in flower,
Copper repoussé box.

Gill Dickinson designed and made:
Child's elebox, Pin-up in silk, String thing, Cactus pencil box, Swish fish, Autumn leaves,
Eggstrordinary Fabergé, Bowtie box.

The publisher would like to thank Mill Store Products Inc., New Bedford, Massachusetts,
for providing blank boxes.